HATS OFF TO
JOHN STETSON

HATS OFF TO JOHN STETSON

Mary Blount Christian

Illustrated by
Ib Ohlsson

MACMILLAN PUBLISHING COMPANY
NEW YORK

MAXWELL MACMILLAN CANADA
TORONTO

MAXWELL MACMILLAN INTERNATIONAL
NEW YORK   OXFORD   SINGAPORE   SYDNEY

To Edna Dill, with love
—M. B. C.

First edition
Printed in the United States of America
1 3 5 7 9 10 8 6 4 2
The text of this book is set in 12 pt. Memphis Light.
The illustrations are rendered in pen and ink and pencil.

Library of Congress Cataloging-in-Publication Data
Christian, Mary Blount.
  Hats off to John Stetson / Mary Blount Christian ; illustrated by Ib Ohlsson. — 1st ed.   p.   cm. Summary: Describes the life of master hatter John Stetson, from his boyhood apprenticeship under his father to his conquest of the American West with his design for the perfect cowboy hat. ISBN 0-02-718465-X 1. Stetson, John Batterson, 1830–1906—Juvenile literature. 2. Hatters—United States—Biography—Juvenile literature. 3. Hat trade—United States—History—Juvenile literature. [1. Stetson, John Batterson, 1830–1906. 2. Hatters.] I. Ohlsson, Ib, ill. II. Title.
  HD9948.U62S743 1992   338.7′68741′092—dc20   [B]   91-34272

CONTENTS

One
AN EARLY START

JOHN BATTERSON STETSON hunched his small, frail frame over the workbench, trying to concentrate on his task, which was attaching the black grosgrain ribbon to the dark gray top hat. He hoped to ignore the distracting shrieks and giggles of the neighborhood children who played in the alley outside his father's small hattery. But it was hard.

Thwack, thwack. He heard the jump rope hitting the cobblestones and knew what was coming next. His ears burned red hot in anticipation of the familiar taunting chant:

> J. B. Stetson, sitting on tacks.
>
> Little Johnny Stetson, making hats.
>
> How many hats did he make?
>
> One, two, three . . .

Nine years old, he had been an apprentice in his father's workshop for two years already. He worked every day but Sunday, his slender fingers stitching or gluing as deftly as any grown-up's. His father would accept nothing less than the best effort.

Schooling was out of the question. "Knowing how to make a good hat that will satisfy a customer is all the education a son of mine needs," his father, Stephen Stetson, said.

"How will John write out an order for a hat if he can't read?" John's mother argued. "How will he move among the educated, moneyed hat buyers if he can't read?"

And so in the evenings, when the workshop was closed and the supper dishes had been washed and put away, Susan Batterson Stetson taught John to read and write, to add and to subtract, just as she'd done for his six older siblings, just as she'd do for his four younger ones when they were old enough.

John ached with curiosity. He wanted to know as much as his brain could hold. "Why is the sky blue, and why is the

wind invisible?" he wanted to know. "What was it like to live in ancient Egypt? And—"

His mother would only smile and say, "I will try to find a book for you with the answers. Then you can read for yourself."

Then John would fall into silence, dreaming of the day he would own books of his own. He would have a library with row upon row of shelves stuffed with books.

Sometimes John wished he could play games with other children. Other nine-year-old boys, even those apprenticing their fathers, got to play outside once in a while. Why did he always have to be here in his father's steamy little hat factory, stitching on hat bands until his fingers were sore and needle-pricked? Wasn't the labor of his older brothers enough?

He sighed. No, probably not. After all, he was one of eleven Stetson children. And although his sister Louisa had already married Hiram Larrick and moved out, his brother Henry would soon want to marry his sweetheart, Susan Campbell, and *she* would move in. They'd be right back at supporting thirteen by making and selling hats. This took the sale of many hats a month. John coughed, trying to clear his throat of the scratch and tickle of the fur dust that was ever present in the damp workroom.

Steam burst from the huge kettle on the stove, filling the air with a shrill whistle and reminding John of his task. He finished stitching the band, then glanced toward another workbench, where Napoleon was deftly shaving fur from beaver skins with his razor-sharp knife.

In 1839 the streets of Orange, New Jersey, were lined with hatteries—there were as many of them as there were blacksmith shops. Yet none worked with a finer choice of animal furs than John's father's. And the finer the fur, the finer the hat.

When Napoleon had finished shaving the fur from the skins, Henry shook them until the coarse outer hairs fell away, leaving only the soft underfur.

It fascinated John that through some miracle none of them really understood, the delicate underfur clung together. The fur formed a tight bond over the cone-shaped mold as Henry continually agitated it over steam.

When Henry slipped the fur from the mold and plunged it into boiling water, it would shrink and become tighter than any woven cloth, even water repellent. It would have become felt.

Then his father's talented fingers would go to work, shaping the felt into a fine stylish hat, curling, smoothing, trimming until it was a perfect top hat or bowler, suitable for the richest heads in New Jersey.

"Don't dawdle, John." His father's sharp reprimand cut into his thoughts. "Idleness is the devil's tool."

"Yes, Father," John replied. He set the finished hat aside and picked up the next.

"Remember, John, hard work and honesty are the trademark of the Stetsons. There is nothing more satisfying than an honest dollar earned."

"No, Father. I mean, yes, Father."

The bell above the shop door jangled. Mr. Stetson slipped into his suit jacket and adjusted his cravat. He pulled back the dark velvet curtain that hung between the dreary workroom and the cheery little shop, where the latest in Stetson haberdashery sat at dapper angles on wooden mannequin heads. Before closing the curtain, he paused to send a stern glance in John's direction.

"Yes, Father," John said, picking up the spool of grosgrain ribbon to measure another band. He glimpsed Henry's friendly, encouraging wink. John grinned at him, then quickly snipped a length of ribbon from the spool, enough to circle the base of the crown, plus one inch. The ribbon had to be just the right length. A ribbon too long or too short would be wasted. And his father did not abide waste. "Waste not, want not," was one of his favorite quotations.

By the time Mr. Stetson returned to the workroom, the light through the western windows had dimmed too much to work by. Henry and Napoleon shut off the fire beneath the steam kettle and stacked the remaining fur pelts for the next day. John covered the unfinished hats with a cloth.

The Stetson men went upstairs, where the smell of stew greeted them. John's sisters, Olivia, five years older than John, and Caroline, only two years older, were setting the table. Martha Ann, who was already sixteen, was watching after their younger siblings. There was George, two years younger than John, Sara Josephine, four years younger, Charles Walter, who was six years younger, and the baby, Elizabeth Amelia.

John's mother placed the tureen of stew and a plate of sliced bread, still piping hot from the oven, on their dining table. The sweet smells were a welcome change from the musty dank smell of fur in the workshop.

"Prepare yourselves for the meal," Mrs. Stetson told them in her prim New England manner.

John shuffled off with Henry, Napoleon, and their father to remove the fur fluff that clung so stubbornly to them.

After supper was John's favorite time. That was when he turned up the gas lamp and settled on the settee next to his mother. He accepted the newspaper she handed him. The newspaper and the Bible—those were his reading texts.

John stared at the drawing on the front page. It showed a man holding a long stick, the fattest part resting against his shoulder. In his other hand he held a ball. John sounded out the words. "Mr. Abner Doubleday conducts the first baseball game in Cooperstown, New York."

Disapproving sounds came from Mr. Stetson's chair in the corner. "Game! A game! What is this 'baseball'?"

John glanced at his mother, who nodded her approval. "Read on, John."

"Men were divided into teams of nine. Each took a turn trying to hit the ball thrown over home plate."

"Plate?" Mr. Stetson said. "These men have nothing better to do than to throw plates?"

"They are throwing a ball, Stephen," Mrs. Stetson said. "They throw this baseball thing over something Mr. Doubleday calls a home plate. Read on, John."

"Mr. Doubleday drew a diamond in the dirt. He called three corners of the diamond bases. The men were to hit the ball, then run, touching as many bases as possible while the ball was in action. The object of the game was to return safely to home plate."

"Harumph!" Mr. Stetson shifted in his chair. "Such utter nonsense! If the object was to be at home plate, why didn't they stay there in the first place?

"Such a waste of time and manpower. Such foolishness. It'll never catch on!"

Two

MOVING ON

Abner Doubleday

BUT BASEBALL *did* catch on. It became second only to the game of nine pins, which was sweeping through New England. It spread all the way to the Missouri River, where the savage west began and civilization ended. At least that's what John read in the *Gazette*.

John found lots of interesting events to read about to his mother on those quiet evenings above the hattery. By the time he was ten, Pennsylvania, Massachusetts, and Connecticut had become states, and the railroad had laid nearly 3,000 miles of tracks, so that people—and news—traveled much faster than before.

"Maybe some of these people will go west, then," Mr. Stetson commented from his easy chair. "Orange is too crowded. It's as if someone left the gate open, and the whole world tried to fit into this one city. Your great-great-great-great-great-grandfather Robert Stetson brought his bride Honour Tucker to Plymouth Colony in 1634 to escape such conditions in England. I'm sure he would not have believed that the same problem would one day plague us."

Stephen Stetson was fond of talking about his ancestors—about Robert Stetson, who rose to the rank of cornet in the armed militia in Plymouth, about Stephen Stetson I, who died at Valley Forge while serving with George Washington. He could trace the Stetson bloodline all the way back to 1605, when Thomas Stetson married Argent Lukesmore in England.

"It says here that there is a law now limiting the hours minors can work in textile factories," John read. He paused. "I'm a minor, aren't I, Mother?"

From his chair in the corner, Stephen Stetson gave his noisiest *harumph* ever. "Now I suppose the little urchins will have more time to run through the streets, begging pennies and picking pockets. Children today have no respect for their elders."

A new story by Charles Dickens, "Olde Curiosity Shoppe," made its way to America, along with four stories by a new writer named Hans Christian Andersen. John read those to his mother, too.

Twice Stephen Stetson became one of the richest hatters in New Jersey, banking more than $50,000, which was a great deal of money then. And twice he lost it all. He decided to sell out his business and retire. The Stetson sons continued to work for the new owner.

Stetson gave his money to a lawyer to invest, and soon most of his money had vanished. It was just as well, as retirement didn't much interest a man who believed that idleness was the devil's tool. Stephen Stetson used what money he had left to buy more hat-making tools and began to work once more. His sons joined him.

But the business was not successful. Americans liked European-made hats; they weren't interested in American-made copies. And with iron steamships crossing the Atlantic in little more than a week now, imported hats were plentiful. Even though John's brother Henry had died in 1853, his younger brothers, George Arthur and Charles Walter, were in the business, too. There was not enough income to support all of them.

John realized that he alone was capable of beginning his own business: He was the best hatmaker among the Stetsons,

and he was not yet married. He decided to break away and try his luck on his own. In 1860, when he was 30 years old, he hugged his mother and sisters good-bye, solemnly shook hands with his father and brothers, and moved to Philadelphia.

There John rented a small room and set up a shop of his own. He had learned his lessons in felting and hatmaking well. He made hats and repaired hats, and he taught young apprentices the trade. When that didn't bring in enough money to live on, he turned to planking—making wooden forms for other hatters.

But a cough that had troubled him for many years got worse. He became thinner, and his hands trembled so that he could barely make a proper hat. His eyes seemed to sink beneath his heavy brows, and his face was gaunt and pasty. Breathing hurt.

Finally, he collapsed in his workshop. His apprentices brought a doctor to him.

"Mr. Stetson," the doctor said, "like many hatters who work in damp rooms with the fur flying, you have consumption, a disease of the lungs. If you don't find a warmer climate, you will not live through the winter. You must leave the hat business to save your life."

"But—" John started to argue.

The doctor shook his head. "It's your choice. But you should think about going west, where there are not so many people and industries. California, perhaps. I hear it is very warm, and the sun is nearly always shining. California is young and unsettled. It might be just the place for you."

"West?" John said. "I'll think about it," he promised.

John's cough got worse. He knew the doctor was right. He sold his tools to his apprentices and bought a train ticket to as far west as he dared go—Illinois.

John discovered that Illinois was little improvement over Philadelphia. Trees were sparse, and the humidity was high. His cough got worse.

"If I stay here I will not see my thirty-first birthday," he told a friend.

Go west, the doctor had advised him. But where? John wondered. Not all the way across the huge continent to California.

The newspapers, which John still read daily, told of a place called St. Joseph, Missouri, a trading post for pioneers heading west over the wagon trail beyond the Missouri River. He decided to try St. Joseph.

When John stepped onto the train platform, his jaw dropped in surprise. St. Jo, as people were calling it, was like no other city he'd ever seen. The main street was lined with hotels, saloons, gambling houses, and churches. Everywhere John looked, he saw people milling about, many of them firing guns into the air. Some of the men were dressed in buckskin clothes, and their hats looked like animals sitting atop their heads—tail, ears, and all!

The Missouri River, which was only a few hundred yards

west of town, seemed alive with hissing, clanking steam-boats. And the air was filled with the braying of mules and the lowing of oxen—and with their stench.

Endless lines of covered wagons stretched as far as John could see over the prairie east of St. Jo. "What are they wait-ing for?" John asked a stranger in buckskins standing nearby.

The man moved his plug of chewing tobacco to his cheek and hooked his thumbs over his low slung gun belt as he replied. "To cross the Missouri, of course. Two ferries work from early morn till midnight. On a good day they can cross maybe 150 wagons, but no more. Since maybe 200 wagons join the line every day, there's no end in sight." The man shifted the tobacco to the other cheek. "You aim to join them?"

John held up his hand. "No, thanks! This is far enough west for me." At least he hoped it was.

Although the hotels were mostly full, John offered to pay a month's rent in advance and got a small, sparsely furnished room. "If you want clean sheets, it's extra," the clerk said.

Exhausted from the travel, John was disappointed that sleep did not come easily in St. Jo. Like a thousand fireflies, camp fires flickered in every direction, turning the prairie orange. Canvas tents and wagons of those who couldn't—or wouldn't—pay the huge price of a dollar a night for a hotel room dotted the flat land.

To make matters worse, it seemed that each tent and wagon contained people determined to sing the night away. The strains of "Oh, Susannah" were lifted by the hot breeze and deposited right there in his room. The tinny sound of organ-grinders rose from the streets, interrupted sometimes by gunfire and voices rising in disagreement.

Groaning, John pulled his pillow over his ears. He finally fell into an uneasy sleep.

There was no sleeping at all past the rooster's crow, when horses, mules, oxen, and people began their push toward the ferries. John washed up and had a breakfast of scrambled eggs, bacon, and biscuits with gravy at the cafe next to the hotel.

Afterward, John set out to explore St. Joseph. He soon realized that it was not just a stopping place for people going somewhere else. It was home to all those people who would make their money selling and trading and serving the pioneers.

It was a booming new city, with plenty of construction work. Everywhere he looked, new buildings—brick buildings—were under construction. Surely with that much building taking place, there was a job for John Batterson Stetson, he thought.

John saw on a door a crude sign that said ACME CONSTRUC-TION COMPANY. He walked right in, tipped his hat, and applied for a job as a construction worker.

The foreman only laughed. "Look at you!" the man said. "You are shaking. This is heavy, hard work. You'd best look for something else."

John thanked the man and left. That was but one opinion,

he told himself. Someone else would feel differently. He strolled along the line of buildings, looking for another construction company.

John glanced at his reflection in a window; he realized he did look pale and helpless. Besides, he was still dressed in his city clothes and his best hat.

John traded his top hat to a store owner for some coarse woollen pants and a billed cap. But he soon found his work clothes did not hide his weak body.

Still John didn't give up. If he couldn't be a bricklayer, maybe he could be a brick *maker.*

Standing on a hillside, John watched men working along the banks of the Missouri River, digging clay with picks and shovels. They were loading it onto horse-drawn carts.

The horses struggled up an incline, dragging their heavy loads to a sprawling brickyard. ST. JOSEPH BRICK, the sign on the largest of the buildings said.

Orange flames leaped, and dark black smoke billowed from huge brick towers, kilns where the brick was baked until it was rock hard. John scampered down the hill to the brickyard. He walked through the door marked OFFICE and asked for a job.

The owner of the brickyard gazed into John's deep-set eyes beneath his heavy brows. "You don't look strong enough. What jobs have you done before now?"

"I've been a hatter and felter since I was a child," John replied. "But I know all about bricks." John did, too, because he'd read their history. "Since their earliest use in Sumeria and Chaldea of Mesopotamia, they haven't changed much. The brick-making process is almost the same today. I know that time and expense can be saved if clay weathers during winter before being used. And I know that you add water before you mold it to make it more pliable and—"

Laughing, the man held up his hand. "Okay, okay, I like your enthusiasm, if not your potential. I'm sure you're not strong enough to harvest the clay. But I'll give you a chance at molding it into bricks."

John squared his chin determinedly. "I promise to work hard and honestly."

Whatever John did, he did with great gusto. And he was always thinking of more efficient ways to do the tasks he accepted. Thoughtfully, he watched the horses struggling up the steep embankment under their heavy loads, the whips cracking and the men shouting to urge them forward.

He went to the owner. "What if we attached the carts to cables running up the incline?" he asked. "What if the horses stayed up here on the level ground, where they would have more leverage? They could use their strength to turn drums that would wind the cable and pull the carts to the top. It would seem a better use of their power, and it would be faster, too."

The owner agreed to try John's idea. When it worked, he was so impressed that he made John the manager.

John saved his money and worked even harder. He went

to the owner again. "I have been thinking about the firing process," he said. "I believe I have a better way to do it."

The owner shook with laughter. "Somehow, John, I thought you would!"

With each improvement John made, the company grew. So did John's savings. Soon John Stetson had enough money to buy part of the brick company. He became a partner. Hard work, his father had told him. Hard work and honesty.

John put every bit of his money into the brickyard. He urged his men on, and after a while, a half million bricks lay in the yard, waiting for firing. The year 1861 would be a turning point in his life, he thought.

But somewhere up north it had been raining, and raining hard. Also, the spring thaw sent melted snow into the rivers and streams. The Missouri River began to rise. The river bubbled and churned over its banks. The water covered the banks of clay. It covered the cables. It covered the brickyards. It covered the wooden molds filled with unfired clay.

The clay turned to mush and was swept away by the river, which looked like churning coffee. The river raged against the wooden molds, smashing them and carrying the pieces downstream. It put out the fires in the kilns and swept away the finished bricks.

When the river subsided to its normal depth, there was nothing left. Overnight, John Stetson had lost almost everything he had to the mighty Missouri. The year 1861 definitely would be a turning point, but not as he'd expected.

John stood on the hillcrest and looked at the empty brickyard. "I'm not the first man to win and lose a fortune," he said, remembering his father. "And I'm still alive to try again. Although not with bricks, I think."

If not bricks, what? he wondered silently.

Three

WITH EACH DISASTER, A NEW OPPORTUNITY

BY THAT TIME, Abraham Lincoln had become president. In protest Alabama, Mississippi, Florida, and Louisiana had formed the Confederate States of America.

Easterners on their way out west brought the news. "Lincoln will never let them get away with it. He's called on our army to suppress the rebels," a man told John as he loaded his wagon with flour and sugar for the journey west. He put his hands on his hips and narrowed his eyes thoughtfully. "Yessir, if more states join the rebs, it means a bloody war for sure."

It wasn't long before the Union opened up a recruiting office in St. Joseph. A soldier with a thick handlebar mustache, wearing a fine dark blue uniform, tacked up notices on every building, asking men to join the army and preserve the Union.

John was one of the first in line. His lungs still ached with every breath he took, and his hands shook uncontrollably as he filled out the enlistment papers.

"My great-great-grandfather was at Valley Forge," John said, "and *his* great-great-grandfather served in the militia in Plymouth Colony. I want to do my part, too."

The soldier leaned over and spread his fingers across the paper, shaking his head. "Sorry, son. I admire your desire to serve. But you haven't the strength to carry a rifle, much less fire it."

Disappointed and frustrated, John left the recruiting office. Outside he leaned against the building, thinking. What was he going to do? His meager savings would soon run out.

The raucous laughter of a group of young men, about a dozen of them, caught his attention. He strolled over to them to ask what was going on.

"There's gold in the Colorado hills!" one of the young men

said. He introduced himself as Moses Johnson. "It's Pikes Peak or bust!"

"Pikes Peak or bust!" the others repeated as they jostled one another good-naturedly.

John smiled at them, recalling the great rush toward California not many years before. A few people had made their fortunes, but most wound up losing everything they owned. They'd headed back east with hand-painted signs on their wagons: "Busted, by God."

"Come with us!" one of the young men suggested. "It'll be a great adventure!"

John shook his head sadly. "I have only enough money left for my next week's rent and a few necessities. I couldn't buy a horse and saddle, much less go in on a wagon."

"Then you have nothing to lose by going, do you?" the one called William Milton said. "We don't have a dollar between us. We're going to walk the 750 miles. And we'll eat whatever game we can kill. And we'll sell or trade most of our clothes for a rifle and a few supplies—pots and pans, stuff like that."

John nodded, admiring their energy and grit. "You know how to hunt?"

Moses shrugged. "Not yet, but we'll learn or starve!"

John cocked his head, thinking. "What about sleeping quarters?" He'd never slept out-of-doors in his life.

William pointed to the sky, where not even a cloud drifted between them and the sun. "You're looking at it. The sky's our roof, and the ground's our floor. The weather is still a little cool, but we'll hang around St. Jo till it turns warmer. We won't need a tent."

John smiled and shook their hands. Nothing ventured, nothing gained. Why shouldn't he go?

Together, they went to one of the many supply stores that lined the streets of St. Jo. They asked the clerk what they needed for their trip, and they talked with wagon scouts to learn what to expect. Meanwhile, they practiced shooting bottles and cans lined up on a stump.

John couldn't help but feel uneasy. "An animal isn't going to sit still on a stump for us," he reminded his companions. "Will we be able to feed ourselves?"

"There are twelve of us," Moses told him. "And we'll have all day to hunt. Surely some of us will hit something sometime. We will swear to share whatever we have, no matter who got it." Moses laughed. "We'll take along some hardtack and beef jerky, just in case. And we can take along some of this popcorn. It won't take up much room, and the old timers swear by it. They say it'll fill your belly but not your pack."

John stared at the hard yellow kernels in Moses' open palm. He'd eaten corn before. On the cob, off the cob, and what they called hominy, all swollen and soft. What was so filling about *this* corn? He shrugged. "Well, I guess they would know," he said.

It was June 1862 and warm by the time the group had organized itself for the trip. John selected a single pair of sturdy trousers, a heavy cotton shirt, and a jacket. He would wear these on the long walk to Pikes Peak. The rest of his clothes he gathered to take to the trading post, and exchanged for a hatchet, a rifle, some ammunition, and a pickax. He joined his new friends at the river. For fifty cents each, they took the ferry across the Missouri.

On the west side of the Missouri River, Moses pointed. "The Platte River Road is a few days southwest from here. And John," he said, "we don't have to walk fast. There's plenty of gold waiting in the Colorado hills. If you feel tired, we'll stop and rest a while."

John knelt and ran his hand across the deep grooves in the bare earth. "We sure don't need a compass to find our way, do we? We can just follow the ruts left by the wagon wheels heading west."

When they had been walking for nearly three hours, John shouted, "Smoke! Something's on fire up ahead! Or maybe it's Indian signal fires!"

Moses cupped his hands over his eyes and squinted. "That's not smoke, John. That's dust, probably stirred up by a wagon train."

"It could be a mile ahead, or ten or more. With the prairie stretching in every direction, distance is hard to judge," William said.

They overtook the group of wagons when it stopped for repairs several days later. "You're welcome to stay the night," the wagon master told them. "We'd enjoy hearing some *new* stories. Old Elijah Beane's stories get a little worn by the fifth telling."

Elijah Beane looked older than the earth, and he said he'd made this same trip twice before. He was the scout. "You stick to the trail, and you won't be bothered by the Injuns," he said. "They's curious, but if you keep movin' and don't shoot nothin' but small game, you'll be all right."

That night they ate corn bread and beans that had been prepared by a Mrs. Abernathy and her daughter Maude, who were going to California to join Mr. Abernathy. "I apologize for the dust in the beans," Mrs. Abernathy told John and the others. "But it's taken these beans three or four campsites to finally cook enough to be edible. Meanwhile, they've picked up a layer of trail dust."

John smiled at her. "They're delicious, Mrs. Abernathy. The dust seems to be the perfect seasoning."

Moses pulled out his harmonica and blew an off-key version of "Oh, Susannah," and the young men, their energy renewed, danced and sang until the fire died down.

The next day the wagon train moved far ahead of them and disappeared over the horizon. The trail stretched across miles of grass that had been grazed by oxen and mules, making the rabbits and prairie chickens easy game. Whenever the men had enough to feed the group, they would stop and make camp.

Sometimes luck was not with them. "It seems every animal

in the west heard us coming today and hid," John said one day. "I hope that popcorn is as filling as the old timers say."

When the fire was going well, Moses poured some popcorn kernels into a skillet and set it atop the fire. The men sat cross-legged around the fire, chatting while their corn heated.

"Shouldn't we use water for boiling?" John asked.

Moses shook his head. "They said it didn't need water. That's one of the beauties of it."

Suddenly, there was a pop! Something white shot past John's ear. "Whoa!" he said. "What was that?"

Pop, pop, pop! White things were flying in every direction. "Quick!" John shouted. "Get a lid!"

Moses slammed the skillet lid down, and the exploding kernels made pinging sounds against it. As they ate their popcorn, the men laughed heartily. "At least now we know why it's so filling," John said.

"And why it's called *popcorn!*" Moses said.

John and his companions killed their game as they found it, carrying it in a knapsack until dusk. Like the wagon trains, they stayed near the rivers so they would always have plenty of water to drink, cook, and wash with. When they couldn't find enough wood for a fire, they would burn buffalo chips, which were plentiful on the prairie and plains.

Eventually, as the ground became more rocky and uneven, the men found an abandoned rocking chair and a wooden chest of drawers. "Probably got too tough for the wagon to maneuver with a full load," Moses said. "I guess when the chips are down, we decide what's really important and what we can leave behind."

"I just hope you don't decide I'm not important enough to keep!" John joked.

Soon after that, they came upon a grave marked only with two sticks tied into a crude cross. John fell silent as he paused, staring at the lonely grave. At last he spoke. "If I die of consumption, at least it will be out-of-doors," he told them. Whatever waited for him, he was ready.

Moses laughed out loud. "*Die*, did you say, John? Why, have you looked at yourself lately? You are suntanned and healthier-looking than you were when we first met. And while the rest of us have lost some weight on our prairie diet, you look as if you've actually *gained* a few pounds."

John grinned at his companions. "You know, I really am breathing easier." He stared at his hands. His pasty skin had turned bronze. His legs felt strong from walking, and his arm muscles rippled beneath the weight of the rifle, hatchet, and ax. He laughed. "I feel a whole lot better!"

The next morning, John awakened before sunrise. He liked watching the sun burst into the sky, a circle of fire. He breathed deeply, enjoying the perfume of the wildflowers and the sweet clover that were his bed. That deep breath hadn't hurt a bit. Surprised, he breathed deeply once more, and again. He *was* getting better! He was sure of it now.

John smiled to himself and scanned the peaceful sight of the sage-flecked plain. The lonely sound of the coyotes at night had been replaced by the thunder-like boom of the prairie chicken males as they courted the hens. How different this was from the cluttered, clattering city with its smoke-smudged sky.

"Ouch!" he shouted and slapped his neck. It was the buzz and bite of the pesky insects that he just couldn't get used to.

On the trail, the young men whistled or sang or joked as they trudged the endless miles, and when they tired of their singing and whistling, Moses would say, "John, tell us a story. Tell us about that rotten old selfish guy Scrooge."

"I've already told you that one three times," John said. "I know lots of Dickens stories. Why don't I tell you about—"

"But we like that one," Moses insisted. "Tell it again, John."

John nodded toward the horizon. While it was still sunny where they were, the horizon had darkened with a mass of rain-heavy clouds. The grass whispered in the wind. The air smelled like an earthen cellar. Sheet lightning flickered at the edge of the prairie, and the air around them suddenly felt chilled.

"The storm will reach us by nightfall," Moses said. "And there's not even a bush to hide under or a hole to crawl in. What will we do?"

"We could make a blanket of the skins from the animals we've killed for food today," William suggested, waving the sack. "If we all work on it at once, it'll be done by the time the storm gets here."

"Let's do it," Moses agreed. "We'll stop here for the day and sew as fast as we can."

So they worked swiftly, overlapping and stitching together the skins—rabbit, beaver, and skunk. By the time they were done, the rain had begun. They huddled together and held the blanket above their heads. The rain beat against it like pebbles, but the men stayed fairly dry.

The next morning the rain had stopped, and the sun came out so hot that steam rose from the wet grass. As they trudged through the prairie mud, John held his hand up to shield his eyes against the glare of the sun. He wished he hadn't traded off his top hat now. Or at least that he'd gotten a hat before he left St. Jo.

"Phew!" William complained around midday. "These animal skins are starting to smell terrible! Throw the blanket away, Moses!"

"Don't think I wouldn't like to," Moses replied. "But there are storm clouds gathering on the horizon again. It looks as if we're in for another storm. We'd better keep our fur blanket."

Eleven voices rose in protest. "I'd rather drown in the rain than get under *that* again," William said. He held his nose. "Besides, we're passing a few small trees now, hickories, I think. Can't we build a lean-to or something?"

"It's too bad we can't weave ourselves a blanket like the Indians'," Moses said.

John smiled as an idea came to him. "But we can! Not like the Indians', but woven all the same."

"You're joshing us!" Moses told him. "You need yarn and a loom for that. Even *I* know that much!"

"All I need are heat, water, friction, and those furs," John told them, recalling his felting days.

His friends shook with laughter. They bet him he couldn't do it. John took the challenge.

"Take 'em!" Moses said, shoving the furs toward John.

"Gather firewood," John instructed. While they searched for firewood, he sharpened his hatchet on a rock until it was razor sharp. With this he shaved the fur from the skins. "I wish I'd kept my hatter's knives," John told his friends as they gathered around to watch. "But this will have to do."

He put the fur into a sieve. Then he cut a hickory sapling and tied a leather thong to each end, bending it like a hunter's bow.

"What's that for, John?" William asked.

"To stir the loose fur, to separate the coarse outer hairs from the soft underfur," John said. "The outer hairs are of no value in hatmaking."

As he stirred the fur, he moistened it with a fine spray of water until the soft underfur clung together.

"Would you look at that!" Moses exclaimed. "Why, it's almost as if that fur had fingers to hold on with!"

"Right!" John said. "If you had a reading glass, you could

see that the fur has little hooks along it, kind of like fishing hooks. That's what makes it cling to itself."

John dipped the sieve into boiling water. As the fur shrank, he squeezed out the excess water until he had a soft felt square. He repeated the process with each fur pelt until he had enough squares for a blanket.

By nightfall, the time when the next storm hit, the men had a watertight tent cover for protection.

"I would never have believed it if I hadn't seen it myself!" Moses said.

As cool and biting as the nights were, the days were hot and glaring. John used the next skins to fashion himself a hat. He made the crown tall, to keep the sun's heat from his head and to allow the air to circulate. He made the brim wide to ward off the sun's glare from his eyes and neck. It looked crude, but it was comfortable.

His companions teased him mercilessly. "John, that's the silliest looking hat I've ever seen! All it needs is a plume or some flowers, and the ladies back East will love it!" Moses said.

William laughed, too. "It's a good thing you gave up the hat business, John. With hats like that, you'd go broke!"

John laughed with them. But mostly he was laughing be- cause his hat was comfortable. It may have looked silly, but it was the most practical hat he'd ever worn.

"Look!" Moses said, pointing toward some puffs of dust

ahead of them. "A bunch of wagons, and they're coming this way."

John looked where Moses pointed. He saw a caravan of freight wagons pulled by teams of oxen. The bump and creak of the heavily loaded wagons and the thump of a hundred or more oxen broke the quiet of the prairie.

John and the others stopped, staring at the sight. As the caravan got closer, John could hear the cracking of the whip. *Whack, whack!* A man riding a horse deftly snapped his long leather whip in midair above the oxen's heads, and the beasts moved forward, bellowing their protests.

"So *that's* a bullwhacker," John said. "Now I see why some people call the freight master that!"

Something on the man's horse sparkled in the sun like a hundred stars. There was a jingling with each step the horse took. When he was near enough, John saw that the man sat atop a fine leather saddle that was decorated with strings of jingling silver conchos.

"That's the most beautiful saddle I've ever seen," John told him when they'd exchanged greetings.

"I bought it in Mexico," the man said, wiping dust and sweat from his forehead. His complexion was ruddy and rough. "We're bringing supplies up to an army fort not far from here." He paused, staring at John's hat. "To tell you the truth, right now I'd gladly exchange this fine saddle for that hat of yours," he told John.

The others laughed. John thought the man was teasing him, too, and laughed heartily. "I don't have a horse, so I don't need a saddle, as fine as it is. I do have a head, so I need my hat."

The man pulled a five-dollar gold piece from his pocket. It gleamed in the sun's rays as he held it in his palm. "I'd like to buy your hat," he said. "Is this enough?"

John stared at the gold piece. He looked at the man. "Are you serious? It's so crude!"

"May be," the man said. "But it'll sure do the job for me out here."

Moses spoke up. "And it's watertight! We have a blanket like it, and it keeps the rain off."

John pulled the hat from his head and gave it to the man. He accepted the gold piece, smiling. That was the first hat he'd sold in years! And it was certainly his oddest.

The men wished one another safe travel. Then John and his companions started forward once more. When he glanced back, he saw that the bullwhacker had filled the hat with water, and his horse was drinking from it.

John burst out laughing. "I guess a hat has more uses than one out here, doesn't it?"

Moses slapped John on the back. "You thought you'd made a hat, John. Instead, you made a ten-gallon felt bucket!"

Four

NEW BEGINNINGS, OLD MEMORIES

THE CHEERFUL COMPANIONS weren't even dispirited when they crossed paths with thousands of "go-backs," men who had given up the search and were heading back East, broke and humbled.

"You'll find nothing but sore muscles and blisters," one disheartened fellow told John.

"We've come with nothing," John told the man, "so if we leave with nothing we'll be none the worse."

The men found the little community at the base of Pikes Peak as noisy as St. Jo, with celebrating miners willingly parting with their hard-found gold dust for a little gambling and entertainment.

The walk from St. Jo had taken months, and the weather was already showing signs of winter. John realized they wouldn't be able to look for gold long, before the snows set in. Yet he felt exhilarated. He had made the 750-mile trip on foot, and he was a healthier man for it. The trip had already been a success, even if he found no gold.

John traded his gold piece for some beef jerky, hardtack, and gold panning equipment for himself, Moses, and William. The others split off to search for gold on their own.

John wrote a letter to his parents and one to his brother George. He wanted them to know that he had arrived safely and how to reach him.

John rejoined his companions, and they headed up the mountain. Soon the sounds of picks and shovels hitting rock echoed all around them. They stood staring at the odd sight. Some men even dug with their pocket knives, trying to free tiny chips of gold wedged in boulder cracks.

John and his friends agreed to meet in the evenings, then scattered to try their hands at finding gold. They'd shared their food during the long trek west. But gold was another matter!

It seemed no time at all before the snow came, stopping

all digging. There was little to do but hole up in makeshift cabins and lean-tos and huddle near the fire.

"It's boring, waiting for spring thaw," William complained.

"But just think about all that snow melting and washing gold down to the streams," Moses said. "John, tell us some of those stories you read," he suggested.

John grinned, remembering some of the Hans Christian Andersen stories that had entertained him. "Once there was a little mermaid who lived in the sea."

"No!" Moses said. "Not *that* kind of story."

"Umm," John said. "What, then?"

"Tell us about hatmaking," Moses said. "That's grown-up."

John laughed. "All right. Did you know that the first hats were made of plaited straw and dated all the way back to the earliest rural communities in Europe and in Asia Minor?"

"Go on, now!" William said.

"And in early statues, Mercury, the messenger god, wore a finely plaited straw hat."

Moses yawned and stretched. "I bet it didn't look anything like that pitiful hat you sold the bullwhacker!"

John laughed and continued. "And in classical Athens and Rome, the artisan class wore a cone-shaped hat that pulled down over their ears and was made of felt. They had a small band around the edge that eventually was expanded into brims, and—"

John shook his head. His companions were sound asleep. With a warm fire on a cold afternoon, they never seemed to hear the end of any story.

John was surprised at how homesick thinking about hats made him feel.

The spring thaw did wash a few nuggets and chips of gold down from the mountains, and it made the trail to town passable. John went to the post office.

"This letter came for you a couple of months ago," the postmaster said.

Eagerly, John took the letter. The return address was that of his brother George. "Dear John," it said. "This is to let you know that Mother passed away on November 24. We buried her in Rosedale Cemetery in Orange. We are all taking care of Father. Take care of yourself, and get well soon. Love, George Arthur."

John dropped into a chair, stricken with grief. He had much to thank his mother for—his love of reading, his belief in himself. And now she was gone. He promised himself that he'd honor her memory by someday doing good for people.

For John and his friends, Pikes Peak held more work than ore. John stuck it out as long as he could, which was 1865. "I'm going back East," he told his companions. "I'm healthy again. Besides, I don't know gold; I know hats. I'll go back to hatmaking."

"But, John," Moses argued, "it was hatmaking that made you sick. You can't do that. Stay with us."

John smiled at Moses. "I feel sure I can make hatmaking a healthier business."

His friends wished him well, and John retraced his steps along the trail to St. Jo. From there, he took a train to Philadelphia. As the train trembled over its silver tracks, taking John eastward, he wondered if he had made the right decision.

The war between the states was over. General Robert E.

Lee, the leader of the Confederate army, had officially sur-
rendered to the Union general, Ulysses S. Grant. Those who
had survived the war were returning to their normal lives. It
was time for him to do that, too.

John visited his father and siblings in New Jersey. "Our
country got its beginnings in Philadelphia, and maybe I can
start over there," John told Stephen Stetson.

With little money to spare, John bought the tools he would
need and rented a room at Seventh Street and Callowhill in
Philadelphia.

He could buy only ten dollars' worth of fur pelts at a time.
He would have to sell the hats he had made from those before
he could afford to buy the next batch of furs.

Once a week, Timothy O'Malley, a big, burly Irishman,
climbed the narrow stairs to John's small shop, bringing a
bale of furs. He would drop the bale onto the workbench with
a thud and hold out his hand for the money.

One week in particular, John paced back and forth. Timothy would be there any moment. John patted his empty
pockets. He had no money to pay for the furs. What would
Timothy say?

Thump, thump. Timothy's heavy boots struck each step.
John wrung his hands, waiting. What would he tell the man?
What would he do? If Timothy wouldn't leave the furs, he
would be out of business.

The Irishman pushed through the door, lifted the bale from
his shoulders, and dropped it onto the workbench. In his

broad Irish brogue, Timothy said, "The old man says you can hold off payin' him a few weeks if you want. Your credit's good with him."

John let out his breath with a whispered "Thanks, I'll do that."

Timothy touched his short, stubby fingers to the bill of his cap and left.

John sank to the stool from relief, his knees nearly buckling under him. But only for a moment. John Batterson Stetson pulled to his full height and said aloud to no one but himself, "I'll make good. I won't breach the trust of the man."

John browsed through the hat shops frequented by the wealthier Philadelphians. Their hats were from Europe. He turned the hats this way and that, trying them on.

Hurrying back to the workshop, he copied them exactly, then returned to the hat shops where he'd first seen the styles. John felt hopeful. After all, his hats were identical in style to the imports.

"What do we want with your copies when we can get one from Europe for the same price?" a store owner asked.

Disappointed, John went back to his room to think. It was the same attitude his father had encountered many years before. Besides, he didn't want his hats to be mere copies. He wanted his hats to be better. One way would be to make his hats lighter in weight. He would make no hat heavier than four ounces, two ounces if he was lucky.

Perhaps if his hats looked a bit different from the others,

he thought, then the public would like them. He made the brim a bit wider than those he'd seen. Although satisfied that it was different enough, John wondered if he could convince store owners to carry such a hat.

As he worked the wet felt into a shape, John smiled, remembering his boisterous, daring friends from Pikes Peak and how they had made him laugh and enjoy life. If he could show that enjoyment in a hat . . . John gave a slight curl to the brim of the hat and cocked it to one side of his head instead of sitting it squarely atop.

When he reached the first hat store, he tipped the hat forward so that it was touching one eyebrow. With a mischievous grin, he strolled briskly into the store, gave a slight twist to his handlebar moustache, as he imagined Beau Brummell would, and touched the brim with his cane in a dapper greeting.

A customer who was in the store at the time smiled at John. "If a hat can make you feel that cheerful on a gray day like this, I want it!" he said. He bought the very hat John was wearing.

"I'll take a dozen of them for the shop," the owner said. It was the biggest single order John had received since he had returned to Philadelphia.

The orders came in steadily, but there weren't enough to make John feel like a success. He worked all day, every day, just as he had in his father's factory. And at night he read the newspapers.

They had stories about how the West was being developed into cattle ranches. He remembered the broad expanses of land fit for grazing. Maybe cattle and land were the "gold" men had been looking for all along.

It was raining when John fired up his steam kettle the next morning. The rain pelting the roof reminded him of that chilly wet night he had huddled under the felt blanket with his companions. He wondered how Moses and William and the others were doing.

John stared at the hat he'd been forming as he daydreamed. The brim was much wider than the others he'd been making. It looked more like the one he'd made on the trail. It would never do for a Philadelphian.

Of course! John leaped to his feet. Those men herding cattle and breathing dust and being pelted by rain didn't need European hats. They needed something made just for them. He, John Stetson, had been there. He had experienced every bit of weather the West could offer. He knew exactly what those cowmen needed.

Five

THE BOSS OF THE PLAINS

JOHN SNATCHED UP the hat and plopped it onto his head. He hurried along the streets of Philadelphia toward a bank that was nearby.

As he walked along the narrow sidewalks, people turned to stare at him and his odd hat. John smiled at them. It didn't bother him that the hat seemed out of place on the streets of Philadelphia. It would look just right on the plains and prairies of the West.

Excitedly, he explained his idea to the banker. "The tall crown will keep his head cool in the summer and warm in the winter. The wide brim will shield his eyes and the back of his neck from the glaring sun or from rain." He smiled. "And it will be perfect for watering horses."

The banker leaned forward, puzzled. Then he laughed as John told him about the bullwhacker.

"Out there in the West, sometimes you can be miles from another human being," John explained. He waved the hat above his head. "But this can be seen a long way off. A man can signal distant riders by waving it. He can urge on his horse by slapping it against the horse's flank, or he can fan dying embers into a roaring camp fire with it."

John tapped the top of the hat. "And he can use it for a pillow at night. It's as soft as eiderdown and as durable as iron."

The banker leaned back in his leather chair and formed a steeple with his fingertips, tapping them slightly. "Will this hat have a name? Something you can use in advertising it?"

John closed his eyes, imagining a proud rancher driving his herd, pushing himself and his cattle to the maximum. "The hat itself will be my advertisement, but, yes," John said, "it will have a name. I'll call it Boss of the Plains."

With the credit the banker gave him, John bought enough
fur to make twenty hats. Into each hat he sewed a leather
label. The label said, "John B. Stetson. Philadelphia." He

mailed the sample hats to stores all over the Southwest, telling them the hats were available for twenty dollars each. He crossed his fingers and added, "I will accept no order for less than a dozen."

Anxiously John waited. Maybe that had been a mistake, insisting on a minimum order. What if twelve were too many? Would anyone like his new design?

He needn't have worried. Soon orders came in, many of them with the money attached and a plea for him to hurry. Within a year his "Boss of the Plains" had won the West.

More and more Westerners clamored for his hats, but they didn't call them by the name he'd given them. They called them "Stetsons." Some called them "John B.'s." Modern dictionaries list Stetson and define it as a hat with a high crown and wide brim.

Soon John's hat was so successful that he gave up all other designs. He was able to send for his father, who lived another 13 years. John expanded his workshop and hired apprentices to keep up with the demand. "Don't ever use an inferior felt or be satisfied with a less than perfect hat," he told his workers. "Remember," he said, "there is no advertisement equal to that of a well-pleased customer."

From his single small room at Seventh Street and Callowhill, he moved to larger quarters on Fourth Street, above Chestnut. There he added another story at his own expense to house the equipment and workers he needed.

Within seven years even that was too small, and he moved to the outskirts of Philadelphia and built five six-story buildings clustered around the area of Fourth Street and Montgomery Avenue. "I want sunshine and fresh air in my buildings," John insisted. "I want my buildings designed to keep my people healthy. Never do I want their lungs to become weak, as mine once were."

John remained conscious of his health and that of his workers. Often he had doctors come to his office. He would send word through his buildings that any employee or member of the employee's family who needed to see a doctor should stop by.

Soon his office became something of a dispensary, and often was jammed with people, making it impossible for him to work. John realized that there was a great need for better health care—and a need to reclaim his office!

He built a free hospital, the Union Mission Hospital, for his employees, their families, and anyone in the community who needed health care. More than 20,000 patients were treated there annually.

John Stetson never forgot his love of books, either. He wanted to make books available to his workers and their families. He built a library and stocked it with 3,000 books. At last he had the library he'd dreamed about as a child.

John believed strongly in the apprentice system in business. "I will begin you at a fair wage," he told young applicants.

"And if you stay through the apprentice period, I will give you a bonus for every week you work. Here is your chance to learn a trade and secure some savings at the same time."

He set up a profit-sharing system and he offered Christmas bonuses for those employees who had worked throughout the year. He even awarded a percentage of the profits to pieceworkers, who were not full-time employees.

He enjoyed meeting with his employees in the auditorium he'd built for meetings and Sunday School. At Christmas he joined them in singing carols and handed out the bonuses personally.

John Stetson had married, and he and Nancy Stetson had one daughter. When his first wife died, he married Sarah Elizabeth Shindler. They had two sons, George Henry and John Batterson, Jr.

John Stetson was generous with his money, but he had not forgotten his New England upbringing. He believed that people should save their money. He also felt that the most stable workers were those who were part of a family, and families needed homes.

Because it was difficult for his employees to buy homes, John began the Stetson Building and Loan Association. And he was always on hand to advise people. "Build your homes with plenty of windows facing south," he said. "Let sunshine flood your homes all year, even in the winter, when the sun is low in the southern sky, and be healthy."

He believed walking was healthful, too. Often he would

stroll through the streets of Philadelphia. And wherever he walked, there were children running after him. John loved to be around children. He laughed and joked with them and passed out quarters, which he kept in his pockets for just that purpose.

John's outer office was almost always crammed with wives of Stetson employees, waiting to show off their new babies. John would step out, chat with each mother, chin-chuck her infant, and give the woman a dollar for the child's piggy bank.

Once he had cleared out one such group, then returned later to a second group. He had greeted all the mothers and children except one, which he eyed suspiciously. "I haven't seen you today, but I am sure I recognize this baby," John said.

Blushing, the young woman said, "I—I borrowed this baby from my neighbor, sir."

John Stetson laughed heartily and gave her a dollar, anyway. "Next time," he said as she was leaving, "make sure the baby you bring is your own!"

With the office empty of visitors at last, John Batterson Stetson stood at his window, looking out over the buildings he owned and the workers' homes he had helped to build.

On the sidewalk across the way, he saw little girls jumping rope, and the words from all those years ago came back to him:

J. B. Stetson, sitting on tacks.

Little Johnny Stetson, making hats.

How many hats did he make?

One, two, three . . .

Millions!

John Batterson Stetson
May 5, 1830–February 18, 1906